Disgusting Body Facts

Puke and Poo

Angela Royston

Chicago, Illinois

www.heinemannraintree.com
Visit our website to find out
more information about
Heinemann-Raintree books.

To order:

☎ Phone 888-454-2279

💻 Visit www.heinemannraintree.com
to browse our catalog and order online.

Edited by Nancy Dickmann, Sian Smith, and
  Rebecca Rissman
Designed by Joanna Hinton Malivoire
Original illustrations ©Capstone Global Library 2010
Original illustrations by Christian Slade
Picture research by Tracy Cummins and Tracey Engel
Originated by Capstone Global Library Ltd
Printed and bound in China by Leo Paper Products Ltd

14 13 12 11 10
10 9 8 7 6 5 4 3 2 1

**Library of Congress Cataloging-in-Publication
Data**
Royston, Angela.
  Puke and poo / Angela Royston.
    p. cm. -- (Disgusting body facts)
  Includes bibliographical references and index.
  ISBN 978-1-4109-3743-8 (hc)
  ISBN 978-1-4109-3749-0 (pb)
1. Digestion--Juvenile literature. 2. Digestive organs-
-Juvenile literature. 3. Human physiology--Juvenile
literature. I. Title.
  QP145.R6925 2010
  612.3--dc22

                                    2009022238

Acknowledgments
The author and publisher are grateful to the following
for permission to reproduce copyright material:
Age fotostock p. **11 background** (©simple stock
shots); Alamy pp. **7** (©Photodisc/Nick Koudis), **15**
(©Phototake Inc./Carol Donner); Getty Images pp. **13**,
20 (©Visuals Unlimited, Inc./Dr. David Phillips), **23**
(©Stone/TSI Pictures); Photo Researchers, Inc.
p. **25** (©Eye of Science); Photolibrary
p. **29** (©Steve Wisbauer); Shutterstock pp. **11
bottom** (©Monkey Business Images), **11 middle**
(©RJ Lerich), **11 top** (©Emin Ozkan), **17 bottom**
(©Tischenko Irina), **17 top** (©Marie C. Fields), **19
bottom** (©ronfromyork), **19 middle**, **19 top**
(©Marie C. Fields), **27** (©Andrey Kudinov); Visuals
Unlimited, Inc. p. **9** (©Nucleus Medical Art).

Cover photograph reproduced with permission
of Alamy (©Poligons Photo Index).

Every effort has been made to contact copyright
holders of material reproduced in this book. Any
omissions will be rectified in subsequent printings if
notice is given to the publisher.

All the Internet addresses (URLs) given in this book
were valid at the time of going to press. However, due
to the dynamic nature of the Internet, some addresses
may have changed, or sites may have changed or
ceased to exist since publication. While the author and
publisher regret any inconvenience this may cause
readers, no responsibility for any such changes can be
accepted by either the author or the publisher.

Some words are shown in bold, **like this**. You can find
out what they mean by looking in the glossary.

Contents

The Food Machine

A long tube joins your mouth to your bottom. It is called your **digestive system**. Food goes in through your mouth. Your body takes in the parts of food it can use. The rest comes out the other end as poo.

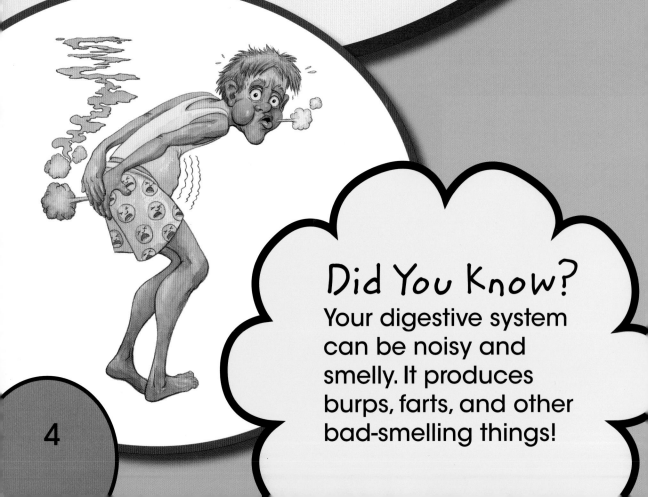

Did You Know?
Your digestive system can be noisy and smelly. It produces burps, farts, and other bad-smelling things!

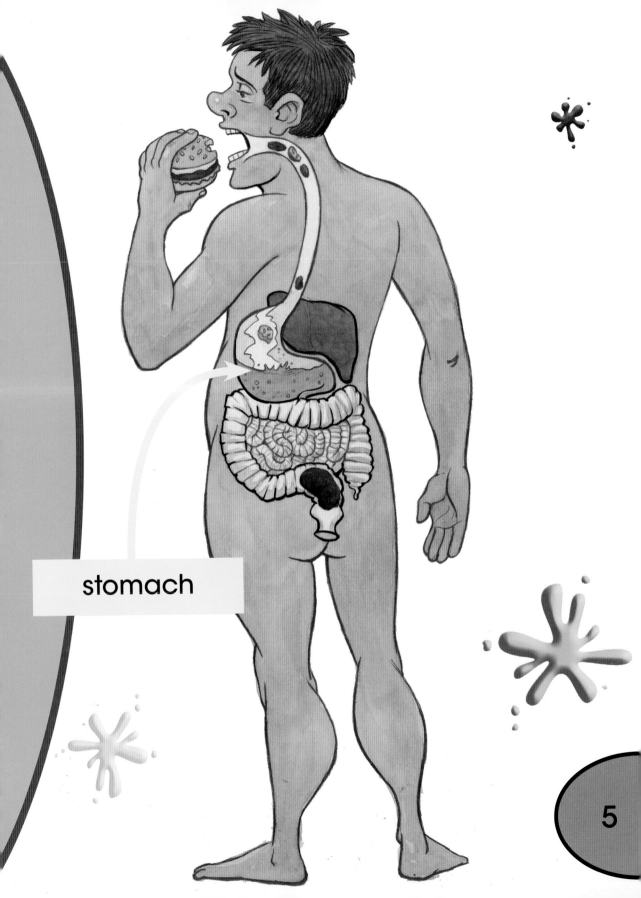

stomach

Puke

Puke is food that your stomach does not like! This is food you have already chewed up and swallowed. Unless you throw up, food stays in your stomach for about three hours.

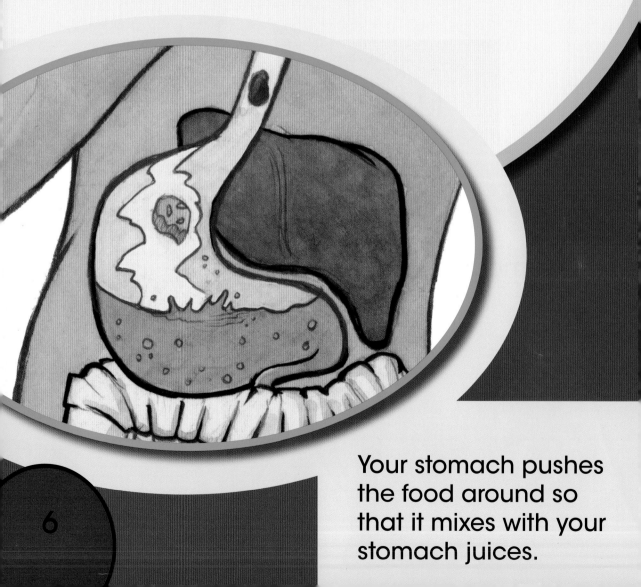

Your stomach pushes the food around so that it mixes with your stomach juices.

puke

Did You Know?
The proper name for puke is "**vomit**." If you want to use an impressive word to describe throwing up, say "**regurgitate**." It means to bring food back up again.

What Happens When You Throw Up?

Your **esophagus** [say "esofagus"] is the tube that joins your mouth to your stomach. Usually a kind of gate called a **valve** stops food from moving back up this tube.

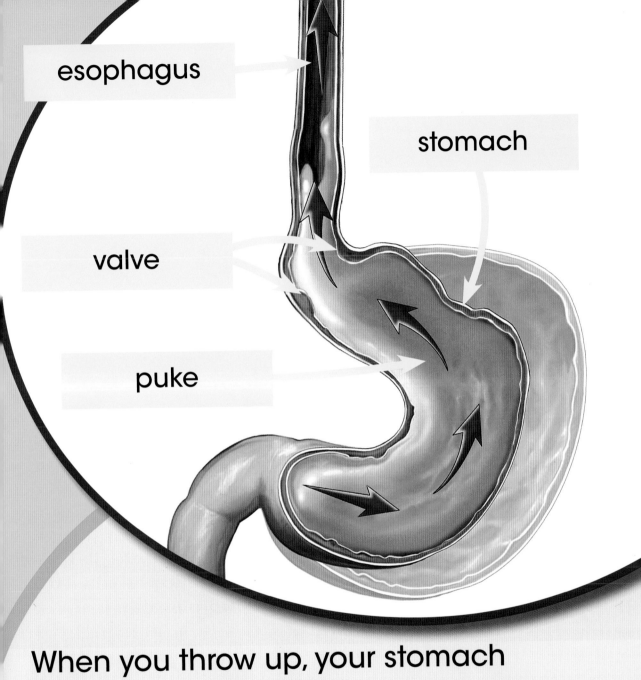

esophagus

stomach

valve

puke

When you throw up, your stomach muscles squeeze your stomach. They force the puke through the valve. The puke goes back up your esophagus and into your mouth.

9

What Makes You Throw Up?

Different things can make you throw up. They include:

- food that has gone bad
- food that was not properly cooked
- tiny living things called **germs**
- eating too much, too fast
- eating something very sweet and fatty
- the smell of someone else's puke!

Did You Know?

Your stomach can hold about 34 ounces of food. That's about as much liquid food as you could fit in four glasses.

rotting
tomatoes

rich, sweet
chocolate cake

under-cooked
meat

11

Why Does Puke Smell?

Puke smells sour because it contains a liquid called **acid**. The acid is made by your stomach. The acid kills **germs** in your food. It also breaks down the food into smaller pieces.

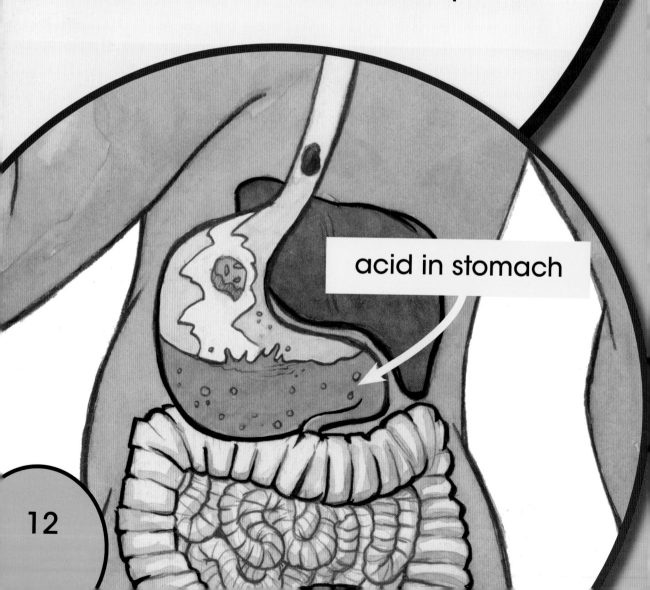

acid in stomach

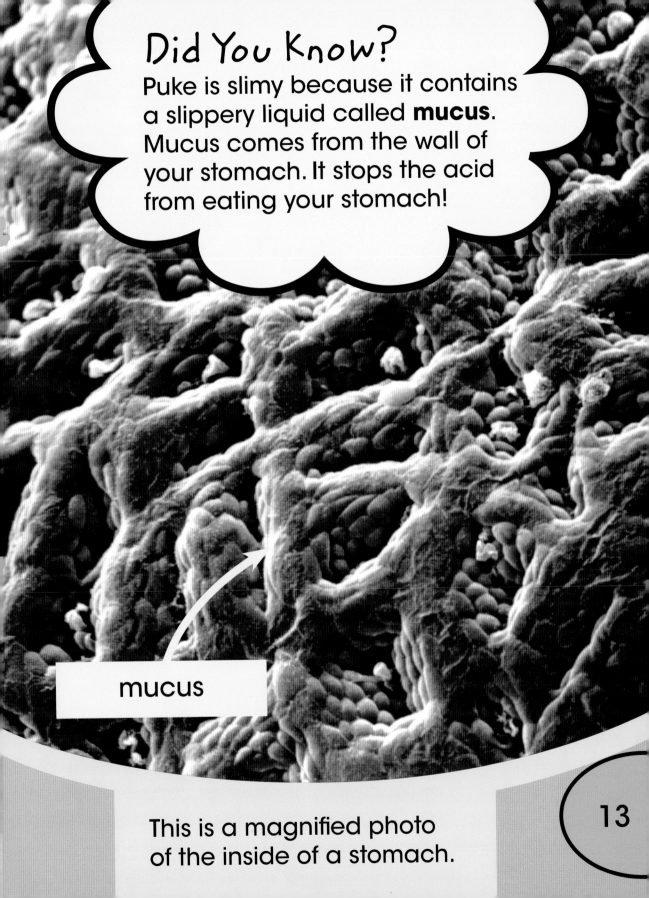

Did You Know?
Puke is slimy because it contains a slippery liquid called **mucus**. Mucus comes from the wall of your stomach. It stops the acid from eating your stomach!

mucus

This is a magnified photo of the inside of a stomach.

Burping

Sometimes your stomach gets too much gas in it. Then the **valve** between the stomach and the **esophagus** opens a little. The gas escapes up the tube from your stomach and out of your mouth. This is called burping!

gas

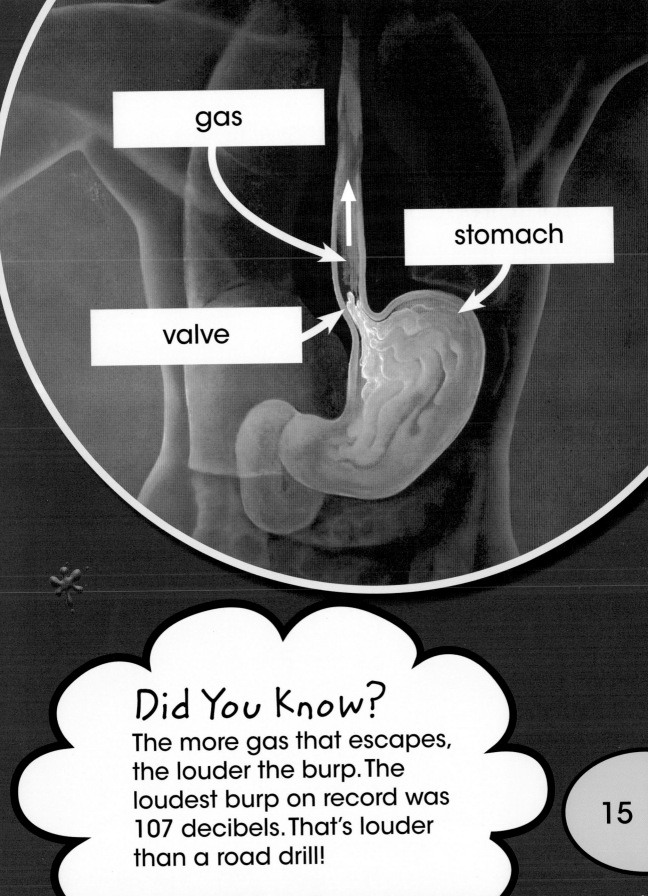

gas

stomach

valve

Did You Know?

The more gas that escapes, the louder the burp. The loudest burp on record was 107 decibels. That's louder than a road drill!

What Causes Burps?

You burp when you swallow too much air or other gas. Soda drinks contain bubbles of gas. A burp often smells and tastes like the food or drink you have swallowed.

Did You Know?

These are some of the things that can make you burp:
- soda
- raw onion
- spicy food

raw onion

soda

Poo

Most of your food is broken down so small that it passes into your blood. **Fiber** is the part of the food that cannot be broken down. It becomes part of your poo.

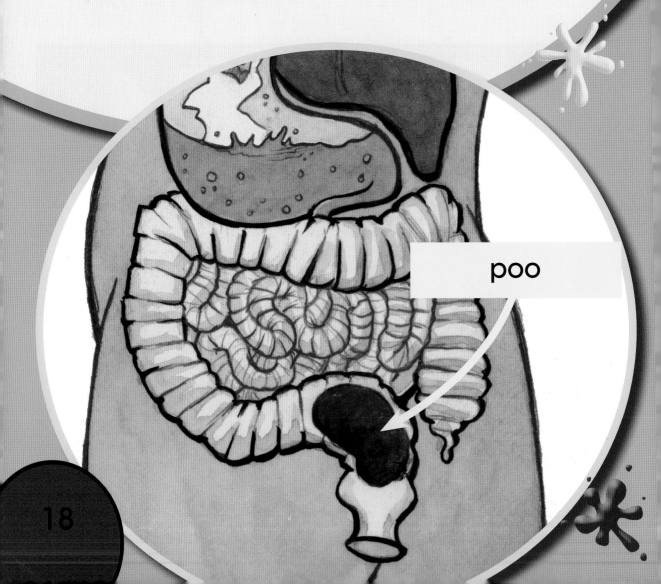

poo

These foods contain lots of fiber.

Did You Know?

Fiber makes your poo bigger and softer, so it is easier to push out of your body.

What Are Farts?

Poo contains a type of **germ** called **bacteria**. Bacteria produce smelly gases. Sometimes bacteria makes too much gas. The extra gas escapes as a fart.

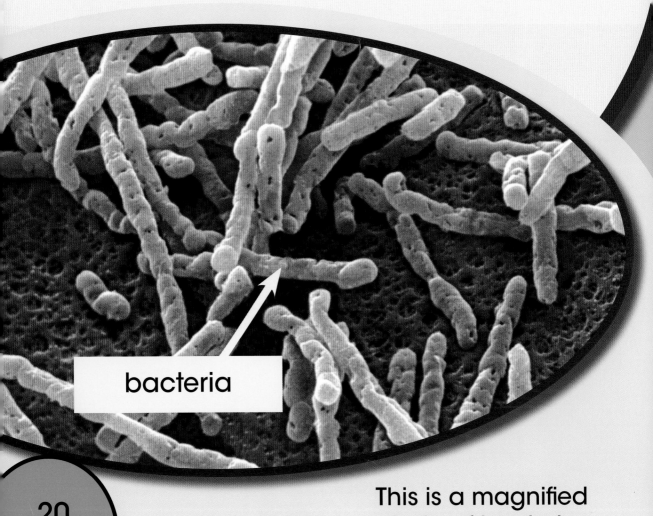

bacteria

This is a magnified photo of bacteria.

Did You Know?
Everyone farts several times a day, but some farts smell more than others. The biggest farts make the most noise!

21

Getting Rid of Poo

Poo moves along a wide tube in your body called the **large intestine**. It slowly piles up at the end of the tube. You push poo out of your body through a hole called the **anus**.

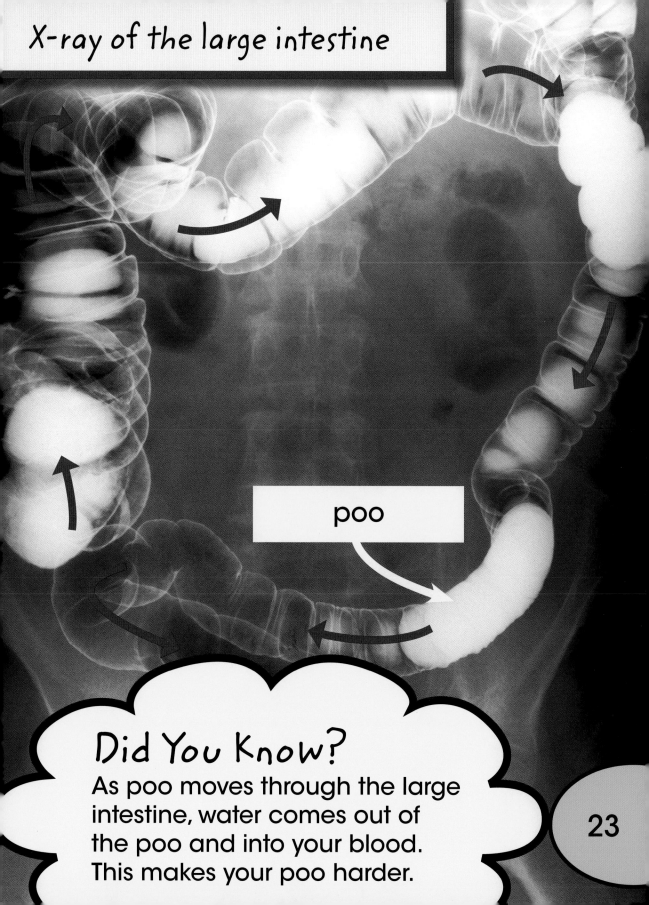

X-ray of the large intestine

poo

Did You Know?
As poo moves through the large intestine, water comes out of the poo and into your blood. This makes your poo harder.

23

Diarrhea

You get diarrhea when your poo contains too much water. This happens when the poo moves through your **large intestine** too quickly. There is not enough time for the water to move into your blood.

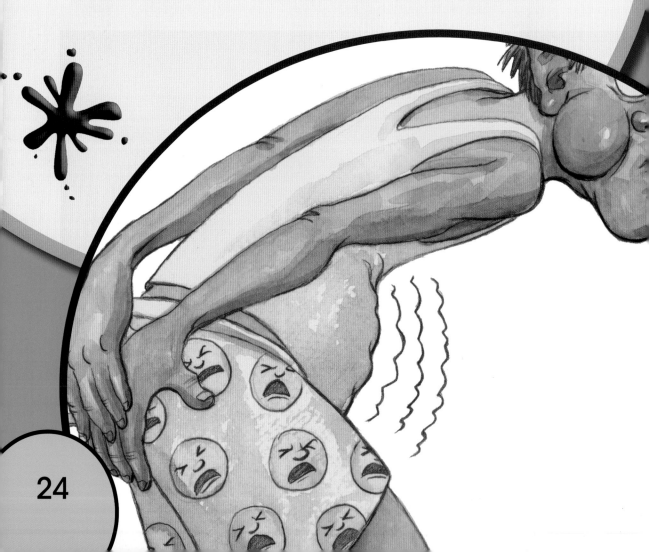

germ that
causes dysentery

Germs can cause
diarrhea. Dysentery is a
type of diarrhea that is so
bad it can kill you.

Constipation

Sometimes your poo contains too little water. The poo becomes so hard it is difficult to push it out of your body. This is called **constipation**. It can be very painful.

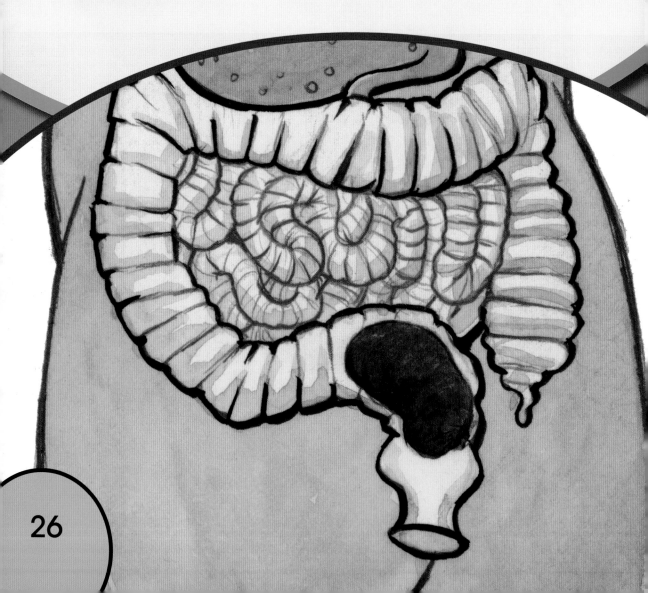

Did You Know?
Camels have incredibly dry poo. This helps them to save water in the desert.

camel poo

More About the Digestive System

If your **digestive system** were spread out, it would be about 5 to 6 times as long as your body.

About three-fourths of your poo is water.

You often get lots of liquid called **saliva** in your mouth just before you throw up. **Acid** in puke can damage your teeth, and the saliva helps to protect them.

Poo is brown because it contains bile. Bile breaks up fat in your food. It is yellow or green. Bile mixes with poo and stains it brown.

Even if you didn't eat, you would still make poo. Poo contains **mucus**, **bacteria**, and dead skin.

Glossary

acid sour liquid that breaks down food and other solids

anus opening in your bottom at the end of the digestive system

bacteria tiny living things. Bacteria are a type of germ.

constipation when poo is so hard it is difficult to push it out of the body

digestive system parts of the body that deal with the food you eat

esophagus tube that joins the mouth and throat to the stomach

fiber parts of food that the body cannot break down

germ tiny living thing that can make you sick if it gets inside your body

large intestine wide tube that takes waste food to the anus

mucus slimy liquid found inside the body

regurgitate vomit or throw up

saliva liquid in the mouth. Saliva is also called "spit."

valve part of the body that works like a gate

vomit food brought back up from the stomach through the mouth. Vomit is also called "puke."

Find Out More

Find out

What should you do if you throw up?

Books

Miller, Connie Colwell. *The Amazingly Gross Human Body: The Pukey Book of Vomit.* Mankato, MN: Capstone, 2009.

Royston, Angela. *My Amazing Body: Eating.* Chicago: Raintree, 2004.

Taylor, Barbara. *The Best Book of the Human Body.* New York: Kingfisher, 2008.

Websites

http://kidshealth.org/kid/ill_injure/sick/puke.html
This Website tells you all about puke and why you throw up.

http://kidshealth.org/kid/ill_injure/sick/constipation.html
This Website tells you about constipation and other interesting topics relating to your digestive system.

Index